MARIN PAUN

TAKE CARE OF YOUR ENERGIES

MEMOIR

SWEETSPIRE LITERATURE
—— MANAGEMENT ——

CONTENTS

Born in Eastern Europe, in a strict family and under a tough authoritarian regime, where authorities used fears to control the population. He decided to immigrate to Australia, a country with free education and free health system. By experiencing addictions such as poker machines he became an authority in addictions. This much helped him in dealing with chronic fatigue syndrome, for nearly twenty years, and that is the extreme chronic fatigue syndrome where people commit suicide. He decided to keep going and focus on the significant contribution, he needs to make to fulfill the mission we are send here for. Personal development is an area of interest to him continuing to be in contact through reading books and following blogs. One area of concern is schizophrenia a condition where 10% of patients commit suicide. Because of this, he writes a book on how to cure schizophrenia, because it is curable, and a lot of lives can be saved.

I need to start from the back to front. What is the current situation. I have a health system which we need to apply for this century and try to get started a socialist movement. It is a socialist as Scandinavian countries and not communism as it might sound. The communist system collapsed 3 decades ago. But there are still left over from the system like e.g., Putin in Russia. I would like to tell you a bit about my childhood because it sets you for life, or at least until something comes to your help. Extremely strict parents controlling and possessive. They put you down, then try to control you: not much development. My father was never home, and my mum accepted him as he was. On top of my parents there was a strict communist system. Where the secret police used fear to control people. Wherever you go, there was dubbing taking place. If you say something nasty, about the people in power, the secret police will know. Later in life I met a girl who was loving and adorable. This was after 9 months in the army. I fell in love with her, she was going to US. Then I decided to leave the country, communist system and my parents. I decided to go with her, but being a boy she dumped me. So I was left with nowhere to go. I decided to take care of my self by being responsible. I decided to go to Australia a country with a free health system and free education, The embassy in Bucharest told me that when I go to Rome, the first thig I should do is to go to the Australian embassy. And I did. After fighting with the secret police, received an approval to live the country. Also I joined the free union and became an activist. This was quite dangerous, they could have hide you. After Rome, I arrived in Australia the country of my choice and not what other people would say. After a few years I discovered psychology, where the self-concept you have becomes yours not your parents or friends you have, Now I can take care of my life. After a few years, my father had cancer. I went back for a few days and I gave him self-esteem. Marriage is not a measure of self-worth. In fact, marriages do not work. After two weeks he was free of cancer. All my life I could not get along with people, but I always have many. The time to get along with people comes in early 40's. But in the same time chronic fatigue hit me, because I was not totally responsible. I was forced to do jobs where I lost energy. The gamble addiction came to my life, which was devastating until I gain control of the poker machines. Just to know we are all addicted. Chronic fatigue is a hard condition and if you do not have privacy and support, you do not conquer it. There are a lot of things going on in my life, but you will all find them in the book. Hopefully you will discover an interesting living, living of a "great".

INTRODUCTION

This book is a memoir but also a book to make people aware to manage their energies in an effective and efficient way. The condition that I suffer from at the moment is called Chronic fatigue and is the worst condition known to the human race and it involves lack of Energies. Leaving Romania in the early 80's under a communist system settling in capitalist Country called Australia.

Chapter I

CURRENT SITUATION

It took one and half years to be diagnosed with the worst condition in the human raceChronic Fatigue Syndrome CFS. In 99% of extreme cases people commit suicide. They Commit suicide because there is no clinic for chronic fatigue, a place where somebody who deals with CFS hard cases, is able to conquer it and developed strategies to deal with it. Currently the condition has started to be recognized especially in big institutions like Hospitals and big clinics. Through a process of elimination, it was established that among Other things like depression and anxiety, I have CFS. We eliminate brain damage caused by other things like alcoholism. Depression was out of question, because after I got out of Depression I was still tired and could not sleep. We use a test designed by the society of CFS and came up with the conclusion that there is CFS.

For the moment my mind is fragmented in pieces and also flat, twice as flat as it should be. I need to use a process of uplifting of the mind, but there are hurdles in the way, like Anxiety layers which block the flowing of energy. Maybe I might not know where the Anxiety is coming from but usually I live in the moment having a day as a measure of time. Now because I am out of the daily living, it probably creates layers on my mind. I have to say that my mind is flat because I met people outside the hours of energy, which are 3-4 hours on top of sleeping. All the rest needs to be spent in bed. This leaves layers of external world to enter the internal world, protection not being there. I have to lift my mind twice, once to bring all the mind together out of fragments and once to get rid of outside layers. To fix the fragments I need a feeling with intense energy on a fragment. This will do the trick (first I have to get rid of the anxiety layers). For the second task, I need good uplifting music which energise you in the same time. Once I achieve the processes of uplifting the mind I need to take the whole system mind, brain, body, spirit, and soul in uniform to uplift to give a sense of wellbeing bringing conditioning which was missing for a long time. Then I can start and live my life. You need to add energies from 30 minutes to 1 hour and 30 minutes every three months. When you reach a level of 10 hours and you know how to manage your energies you will be out of the danger zone. I was on 10 hours energies but because I could not handle energies I went back to 3 hours even 0 hours. The above material you will not find anywhere. You will not find it anywhere because there is not one person in Australia who has reached this stage of fragmentation and uplifting and recover, from this plateau. Anyway, there is a beginning for everything.

For the moment I see the GP (general practitioner) once a month and the psychiatrist once every 6 months. You might wonder why there is a need for psychiatrists. The GP is not good at dispatching of medication for anxiety or depression. When I was with one GP he put me on Efexor an antidepressant and antianxiety drug, on a full dose. I could not walk for 2 days. So, I prefer the psychiatrists to prescribe me my medication and see the GP to provide me with the scripts and at the same time to ask me if I am well and not suicidal. All my medications come in a weekly package known as a webster pack and is delivered by the pharmacy as it has been for 6 years. Well just because I know what to do it does not mean that I can do it. I have very strong layers anxiety of which so far, I cannot get rid of .

At the time of CFS condition I thought it was a body condition, that is because I lost 20 kilograms of mass following fearful panic attacks. On T.V. they said that a guy who travelled to the south pole, lost a lot of mass and died. So, I believed the same thing that protein was the problem. Any condition thrown at me I believe I can cure, so there was no fear because of CFS I thought for 2 years and then I would be able to re-enter society, I was wrong it was very hard to find privacy at an affordable place to sleep. Actually, it is hard to find an affordable place to sleep let alone the privacy. For me screaming and playing guitar was part of privacy. You can obtain a place to sleep from the government, but never have your privacy. Usually these places are negative in the sense that everything seem to be destructible. People scream, people are on drugs and all sorts of things which do not make life more pleasurable.

All my life I used to live in low level of energy. People used to say you need fibre. The problem was much deeper. Being surrounded by friends, made my psychological problems come to the surface late in my life, at the age of 33. Any way, you are never old enough to change, with psychological support you can change at the age of 50.

The whole purpose of this book, apart from the memoir is to show people that no matter how much energy you, have, you need to watch it, you need to manage it. I started this book with chronic fatigue where the energies were at 12 %. of the battery. Apart, from 2 years in my life where the energies were at 85%, most of it was a poor level of energy. This comes from the fact that nobody showed me how to save energy or how important energy is in someone's life. Start with the 'boring' sleep, chase quality of jobs and then put yourself in situations where you can get energy and do not lose too much.

You are always responsible for your life, totally responsible so I can only blame myself for the situation I am currently in, CFS and other problems. But the qualities of jobs were not there, the last challenging job being in 1996 with BOC gases. The job platforms and the affordable renting was not there, and if you are very sick it becomes the responsibility of the doctor. You can no longer be responsible. The whole health system seems to me, has no responsibility on the doctor but the 'center' of doctors. Everything spins around the doctor. Despite of whatever everybody is saying, even if we are one of the best in the world, the health system is not existent. There are people who have ideas on how to fix systems, we only need to advertise of what we want effective, efficient and transparent health system.

I have to mention here that whatever the experiences we face, it will make you a stronger, more tenacious individual, ready to achieve the mission and make a contribution to the world, and the more significant the better.

Where I am at the moment I can say I have tranquillity through a number of people 5 (not 8 from the previous accommodation), and the fact that we are all getting along , despite some people not liking the gay. I try to keep the house in harmony. You can be easily kicked out of the property because there are 30 people waiting to take your place. So, a little mistake and you are out on the streets. The only place you are secure is the negative government place and the house you fully bought (you cannot be kicked out of your own house). Also, I have some friends who helped me a bit, I do not have a friend which I can rely on in any circumstances. This makes life harder than it should be. I have some financial help from my parents even if their pensions are less significant than the one in Australia. It is easier for them because they have their own house and all live all together. Apart from the group of friends you have in your life which you can rely on, the right people, you need to travel well with the super conscious mind, (the ocean of infinite intelligence).

At the moment, sometimes I feel like giving up. The thought of 'I can't' keeps coming up. It looks like the spirit is playing up. I use will power to get me through the situation. I have to remind myself that it is a tough situation and not easy to deal with, but it is winnable.

I always tried to do a lot of things in my life, but I was never able to achieve them. I think if I stay alive, I would be better off this time because of experiences which I have. In, contrast my family never tried to do anything, always trying to put the blame on other people, My parents and my aggressive sister are unidimensional They do things because they have to and they only know the game of numbers. We are totally different, I live on principle. I try to do too many things. You can only do between 2 and 4 things at a time, otherwise you will be overloaded and you have anxiety attacks to deal with them.

'The process of death' is a process on the development scale which takes place after the acquiring of self-esteem, that is 3 years of development. I acquired mine if you can say so, from a book written by someone who conquered cancer of the chest. Instead of living scared of death you live because of your mission. A mission which you need to find out what it is if you do not know it. I know mine, so I live because of them. There is no need to worry if you do not know your mission. You are on a path to finding it. Jimi Hendrix used to have a song in which he asks people to "come alive', that is what he means is wake up and live your life of finding a mission. Only 10% of people have been through the process of death (or the process if life), only 10% of people are awake. With extreme CFS we need to accelerate a lot of processes, there is no time for complacency, there are many situations where your life is in danger. And you can manage that because you have been through the process of death. Acquiring self-esteem needs to be done in 3 to 6 months and as I said all the processes need to be accelerated. The process of death is 3 to 6 months of extreme chronic fatigue. Now you can imagine how you become a master of internal world. By doing things over and over again in a short period of time. With the anxiety I currently have I would not be far away without Valium. It makes me sleep which gives me energy, and reduces the over anxiety. It gives me the chance to follow the government for the next health system and any other ideas. The first answer I got from the government was 'we are into making the mental health more accepted by people'. This covers mental health. More pain and more suffering for people. Other answer was 'I am writing things down' and that was all.' A lot of people are suffering and if we do not implement the system is more pain, 'We are impowering people to get well outside the hospitals'. If this works this will produces people with 10,15 or 20 years of pain. You have a superconscious solution (the ocean of infinite intelligence) which means this is the system for the next 100 years. A better answer with no guarantee is to introduce it in 2018 elections. Another answer 'is to keep an eye on it while the elections will come'. This is another 1 and half years of suffering. Some people would say you should be happy you have got an answer. Well, I will take it to the Scandinavian countries and see what they say.

From here on you will see the road, the life, the experience, of a journey taken by me and to become the person I am. I will do my best to emphasize the best or the worst part of the journey because apart from other things life is a journey.

CHAPTER II

CHILDHOOD

I can only remember years from my early childhood, not all which helped me become the person I am. My mother, my father and my sister living in the same one-bedroom apartment in central Bucharest. I remember me and my father boxing figuratively. Me and my sister climbing on a table, on a bicycle to get to the top of the wardrobe. And then going to bed as soon as we heard my mum and my father coming. Also, I remember being in the apartment at 3 o'clock in the morning witnessing how my father would punch my mum in the stomach. There is also a picture of me where I was bubbly and gregarious at the at the of 3, something which cannot be said in the picture at the age of six. Leaving in Bucharest Central I start going to school at the Age of six. I do not know if I was excited, but it was the first day of school. I was going to last for only a semester because there were new housings for the family. I was asked to read something, and I have not done a good job. The teacher quickly said something nasty and the children all laughed. That set me up for life for a public speaking fear thinking that people are looking at me. Although I can currently fix it, it is a fear of people looking at me when I make mistakes. It can be fixed but I do not consider it to be very important. What I remember are fragments from my childhood, I used to play with children of my age and got hit with a pole between my eyes, it was my luck it did not enter my eyes. That required a time to heal and I remember that. I have also remember cleaning a car, the owners gave me a trumpet.

The time to play in the center of Bucharest was over, and we moved to a 3 bedroom apartment at the periphery of the town. The primary school was changed, and I met new friends. Also there were 200 apartments in the block and another 400 in the neighbourhood. Imagine how many kinds of friends you can have.? Children in primary school used to fight a lot. I was picked on by a guy, bullied by a guy, punched and pushed around. I had to fight back, that was the only way I could stop him. I do remember telling my parents, but their child is not like that is what they said. I remember playing soccer in other blocks or other part of the sector. This was an activity which filled up my spared time. I was not good at soccer, but I could run and that made me a good defender. With that I got to play for big clubs. After numerous runs around the stadium and not much soccer I decided to give it up. Another sport that I tried and was not good enough at, was table tennis. I was close to getting admission, but it did not happen.

In high school I was surrounded by people from the country. In mathematics that, I liked I was one of the best. I could never be in school without mathematics and culminated in a statistics degree. In my childhood I had a lot of friends but only recently I started to get along At the time, the game of numbers which you need to get along with people, was missing. I was always withdrawn in childhood and made up my childhood with close relationships. In high school I used to get paid and it was good because I could afford an electric guitar. At the second attempt I started playing. First one being at acoustic guitar and playing only waltz The second attempt I started to play was the time between the university and army. Every time I was lonely I used to have the guitar and that proved to be a valuable asset. Something which I did not realise until I got late in life. I could not play in a band but could play for people I surround myself with.

CHAPTER III

GROWING UP WITH STRICT PARENTS

T here is definitely a difference between a 3 year photo old and a 6 years old photo. I go from a bubbly happy personality to one which is depressed and sad. The absence of my father in my early life and my life in general produced anger in the system because I could not get the attention and love from my parents that I needed. In particular my father who was never home and always the pub every day. Later in life I have found that he did not like my mum, my sister and me. The house was for him to impress people at the pub or his friends. Such a small world. My father was going out with other women and of course he had to fight my mother. He also used to speak rudely to her in front of other people. All this life we took my mother's side because she was always home. It did not make any difference to her, she still loved him as he was. Something I could not comprehend. Even these days he asks me why I took my mother side. That was obvious. There was never the raise of self- esteem, the quality of a relationship, the link of the families.

My mum was grown up by my aunts. Her parents died young at the age of 24 and 31 respectively. She did not have the love required for a human being. She was also grown strict with fears and the impression that the world is a dangerous place. At the time I write this material my father had been dead for 4 weeks, he died at the age of 91. In the end both of them started to live their lives through their children, it was the best solution, if we cannot do it the children will do it because everything is genetic. The parents never believe in themselves let alone in our selves. Never believed that I could go to the university, I can go to Australia, that I know why I am doing and what I am doing. Every time you wanted to get something from them you needed to break the windows, and I did. They only give because they have to. My sister is still under them, under their thumb. She devoted whatever life she had to them. One thing I was getting from my parents it was money. Money to go to the university, money to go to Australia, pocket money to go out with friends. I think I should mentioned that if it was not for their generosity I would have probably being locked up for life in the country's jail.

I got sick while with them, at the age of 12, I got nephritis an infection of the kidney because I could not get the required attention from them, it was really serious. I was told I am not going to live. After 2 years of attention my condition cured partially. I have a smaller kidney which stopped functioning and a larger one which renal functions is not that good. I did not believe whatever the doctors told me and continue until the age of sixty with my own kidneys. A bit of dialysis machine and a kidney transplant, would do the job. Growing children takes a lot of effort and if you are not going to put in to your children maybe is better not to have them.

One thing I want to say is that my parents want the children to do things for them. Marry for me. Do such a job for me. I want to know and meet the people you are going out with. I want to know that your life goes in the direction we want. This is something which I can never agree upon because to be happy requires freedom. Everything you will give away from you, you will feel more and more unhappy. This is not what a relationship is about. I will fight anyone who tries to use me, and this includes my parents. My parents were in control parents. Who knew everything about you including girlfriends.

CHAPTER IV

STRICT COUNTRY, CEAUSESCU, ROMANIA, SECURITATE

About Romania, under Ceausescu one of the strictest countries in eastern Europe where everybody was led with an iron fist. The division followed the division of Europe by the English, Americans and Russians at Yalta in 1945 There was never a desire of the Romania to have a dictatorial regime, it was imposed by the Russians. There was dictatorial experience from Marshall Antonescu who was getting on well with the Germans, being the preferred one in front of the Iron Guard, which was a fascist movement. Also in power was The King, who was in dialogue with the English and the Americans. Later when the Russians would conquer the country he would be sent in exile to Switzerland.

There is a lost love between eastern Europe and the Russians. Even these days when they are free from an evil system they still talk about, the Russians are not to be invaded by them. Recently 2017, Russia and Belorussia conducted military exercises at the border with Poland and the Baltic states. There is a danger of the Russians getting in the country with troops again.

One little escape is the fact that all the eastern European countries have joined NATO, an alliance where if one country is aggressed on by another, all the countries will jump in for help. Any way the Russian system produced throughout eastern Europe and other countries, dictators who would put people down and manipulate them with the secret police. As well as police supervisions the government was using spies to keep an eye on people, you could have been married to someone who is a spy. We all kept an eye on each other so if something was happening the secret police would intervene and eliminate the danger. This system and policy would end with the realisation that you cannot be dictator for ever.

After the collapsed of these dictatorial countries throughout Europe, the experience in democracy was not there. Democracy needed to be embraced from the beginning and experimented on. A lot of problems would arise because the European Union has to be built as well. I do not believe that the capitalist system is good either, it has collapsed in 2008 with the rise of financial crisis, the biggest crisis since the depressions of 1930s. I am a firm believer in freedom, and the only freedom you have so far is at home. Capitalist system produced recessions because there are a lot of problems. Also, most of the wealth is in the hands of a few, top 1%, and you are a bit free to run your life. I believe you should have an education system and health system which is right. A transparent financial system. The Democratic systems has its own flaws and the best and only system is the Swedish Socialist system and slowly and slowly we converge to this type of system.

Under the "socialist" system which you will find in North Korea, you will have a job, holiday, a cement box and food on the table. You will also go on Holiday every year. Most of the TV is about the leader and if possible some sport and music. You will also have an ID card, you can not be in a group of 3 or more. The army works with police together in groups patrolling the streets. A health system is provided together with the education for free, the rest not being transparent. Surely this kind of behaviour would not last and that is why it collapsed. Boredom must be another factor together with computing to affect the collapse of the "socialist system".

Much later after I left, the people would find hard to find food, because Nicola Ceausescu had to pay back money he borrowed, from the Western Countries. So, there was a period of famine especially if you did not have anybody with connections in the food industry.

When I was there up to 1981 there was no shortage of food, you could go to restaurants, and holiday spots. You were not allowed to see any of the musical groups from the 'west". The secret police were everywhere and at a sign of trouble you would disappear and never be seen again. So strict everything was. It is believed that after 8-10 years as leader you become addicted to power and it gets in to you and you lose touch with humanity. Since Nicolae Ceausescu was in charge between 1965 to 1989, 24 years, it makes sense that he lost touch with people. He was eventually shot by a firing squad mainly because the new system did not want a war between his forces and the new people. I remember being very close to him when I was in High School, when we were invited to international exhibitions. All his associates in power used to set up meeting with people when he was out, people who would "adore him". From my point of view everything was done with force and it did not turn me on to adulate him. Among other eastern Europeans, Ceausescu regime was most stringent.

CHAPTER V

HIGH SCHOOL, TERTIARY EDUCATION AND ARMY

T o choose a High School, as spoken before, needs to have mathematics as subjects otherwise I would not do it. Romanian language at the time was something untapped. I enjoyed cars and a High School to become good in mathematics and physics was a good thing. I had to sit exams if there was a high demand. Between the VIIIth and IXth forms there were no high demands so the exam was not required. In the forms Xth and XIth again there was no demand so I did not sit the mathematics and physics. Also, the high school is technical, producing mechanics I did not have anything to do with that, I wanted to do university in automotive engineering, and I was always interested in physics and mathematics. Following exams, I was the only student form High School to enter the faculty of automotive engineering. And my parents did not believe in me.

The exam acceptance reduced my military service to 9 months from 16 months Once I finished the military obligation I would be assigned the rank of sublieutenant and in case of war lieutenant. Other people have their own thing to do and I would play guitar in summer prior to army. A special case was made of wood and I went to the center of military recruitment. I was assigned close to the Yugoslav border in a town full of army and less civilians. Despite that I missed my family and friends in Bucharest, the first 3 months were full of training and were good. It was a lot of shooting, parade, cleaning, physical exercise, amphibious vehicles, and all sorts of activities which made you become a good soldier. Again, the first three months were good, but the rest was a waste of time. We were mostly used for guarding the premises, also going home for a period of time and spending time with the people you love was a priority. To go home you needed someone high in ranks, so they will obey. It took me a while to find someone with ranks. Some people were going home every weekend. Others like me not so much. I remember this period of life being with 6 months of time off. And some knowledge in the army.

Starting university was different from high school. You are seen as an equal to the lecturer and assistant lecturer. You can grow hair and that is what we wanted. You can dress well and you are seen as a future engineer. Anyone who finishes university has a place allocated to work. And in order of marks you can pick your job and town.

Something which I always be against is the segregation of women versus male. In high school there were few females but in university there were plenty, I believe women and men need to be mixed in education to experience the company of the member of the opposite sex.

About this period of time, I remember that I used to drink with friends, a lot of beer and cabernet sauvignon. A period of drinking was there because there was a lot of free time. It covers the army as well, where we knew a lot of wine producers. In university you would drink at the parties, the rest of the time you needed to study. Now because my father was an alcoholic I would never drink as much as him, and would never allow the alcohol to be my addiction.

CHAPTER VI

LEAVING THE COUNTRY. SECURITATE.

L eaving Romania for the west was going to happen, very important chapter in my life. As I mentioned there were plenty of parties at University and in one of them I discovered the love of my life. She was 3 years older than me. All my life I enjoyed ladies which were younger or older, never my age. The reason being, that I look in the mirror everyday seeing myself of same age, over and over again. I felt strongly about these women even if there was an age difference. She was a photographer. She loved black and white photography and she had her own exhibitions. It was an infatuation which lasted for a while.

I have found out that she was leaving the country for the USA. Also, her friends were leaving the country for Holland, Canada and USA. It was legal to leave the country because of the conditions put when burrowing the 22 billion dollars from USA. You have to let people go.

Once a week you would be meeting with the Securitate (secret police) and a member of police to discuss the status of the passport application. It was named the small forms. Once you are approved and got the big forms you were on your way to the passport and to leaving the country for the USA. I was not sure about the relationship with Jimi, that was her given name. I knew the relationship would not last, but anyway I took my chances and decided to leave the country too, even if in the back of my mind there were no assurance we would be together then it happened, she dropped me one week before going to America. Despite my expectations of not lasting, I was still hit by a "train".

Since I asked to leave the country, the friends I used to have from university, block of flats etc. would not socialize with me. All of the sudden I was isolated and the only people I had as friends were people who would like to leave the country. The brother of a friends of Jimi's became my best friend. I was knocked out of the university, I was chased for not working, for which you can be put in jail for 6 months. On the other side you were not allowed to work.

To boost my chances of a passport I went on hungry strike. After 11 days without food I gave it up because nobody would be interested. Then I tried to lock myself and my friend in the Canadian embassy even if we did not go to Canada. In the end the Canadians said no so we had to leave the embassy. 2 minutes after we left, Securitate turned up. We were close to disappearing for ever. We went to the border with Yugoslavia trying to jump the border. A country which gives back refugees and not depending on their mood. Ceausescu would give them a wagon of salt for their return. I joined the free union movement, an organisation that tried to bring free union in the country. We declared another hunger strike for us and the people in the union. I did not believe we would have any effect because of my previous encounter. So, I was not bothered by the new hunger strike. It was advertised through radio free Europe and got the Securitate upset. I had 7 guys at my door, trying to pick me up and put me away. I ran away and moved around Bucharest for 3 to 4 months together with my friend, without being detected. The idea was good it took the steam out of the situation. It was easier to deal with the Securitate. My mother had a cousin who had high rank in Securitate and said whatever they were doing was not legal. He was at counter espionage equivalent to MI5. That helped. It shows how various parts of secret police used to work to keep an eye on each other to keep themselves in check. We gave ourselves up and in 2 days, after many questions we were released.

This is the period when I myself become a spy. Following the meeting between myself and colonel of Securitate, I signed papers that I would keep an eye on the guys from Police boot for passports. I thought that would make my departure faster. In case something was going on at the station, like movements I would not have given up and I put myself in the line of fire. It proved to be more time consuming with no rewards. Nothing happened, and I went to the Ceausescu Advisor Bureau. Once the colonel heard this he relieved me at once. So, I had the big forms but he would not release me. The colonel after years later, tried to contact me in 1994, I know that ASIO knew about my contact. He was probably looking for some help to get out of the country because the regime it was defeated. I never believed that I was a spy. If I did not want to be a spy there is nothing they can do to force me to be a spy. As far as I am concerned the connection finished there at the Securitate meeting, there is nothing to spy in Australia, I was too antisocial, withdrawn and shy to be a successful spy.

For me this period was hard, I had cold bones, it felt that my mind was not working properly, it was almost like giving up. I also became deaf which is psychosomatic. I felt lonely all the time, I lost my friends, did not have any friends in the country. My parents were against me they did not believe that I could leave the country. I had the Securitate on my back, until that plane would land and see me on Italian soil. That is because on the plane, there were Securitate and sometimes they would hold people and make them disappear. The level of energy was low and I always felt cold, I was sleeping a lot which was good and another good point is that it was temporary condition. Finally, after 1 ½ years of applying for a passport I was issued one. It was brown in the colour and that meant I had to give up citizenship. And I did it because the passport was more important.

I want to say that my departure would open the door for more people to leave the country. People who had relatives, people from the block of flats I was living in, and this was before the Ceausescu's regime would fall. These days there are a lot of migrants on skills who are leaving the country but not refugees.

Chapter VII

ARRIVING IN AUSTRALIA VIA ROME

I managed to arrive in Rome, without any problems from the Securitate whatsoever. I have also had a friend who went to the USA. With this new friend I was introduced to Italians families, I would go out with them and see their businesses.

They gave us a small hotel where everything was provided. Everything was handled by Agencies, I went via Rome main train stations and there were people sleeping on the floor, without having a place to go and sleep. I was not impressed at the first sight of western countries. My friend was going to the USA so, our friendship did not last a long time. I exchanged my details with him but I did not reply, he will only know about me because I was going to Australia to cover up in case he was not successful in the USA.

As per conversation we had in Bucharest with the Australian embassy, if you want to go to Australia, go straight away to the embassy, not American and I did that. I know of some people who wanted to go to Australia but they first went to the USA. The visa was denied by Australia. The American embassy was not too impressed when I did not appear at the interview. While in Rome, I worked as a tourist guide assistant and made some pocket money to pay for the expenses, while waiting for the place in camp. I remember the heaviness of the luggage. I was put in to a camp in a town called Latina, and it was close to Rome. The Camp in Latina was rough. Every night the nationalists had fights. Women were raped and there was only one policeman. How can one policeman keep order? The locks at the door were missing, the food was good and plenty. There were demonstrations in Rome to make the Latina camp more safe and secure. I started doing some part time work. The first job was to lift haystacks from the field on to trucks. I did not last 5 minutes. The haystacks were full of water and heavy following the rain. The next job was in constructions, assistant bricklayer, much better lasting for a while. In terms of expectations of capitalists where everything was big and happiness was everywhere, Italy and Rome, did not have it. There were people on the street, the camp was hard for a lot of people especially women. I was supposed to wait 3 to 4 months until I would be flown to Australia by Qantas. I was sent to Napoli, a change of camps. A much better proposition. It was the home of cosa nostra where the carabinieri was fighting the mafia. Everything was in order. There were locks, order and police and security at the door. Not much to do apart from eating and picking tomatoes from the field. The 3 months of waiting have come. Australia was better but still not as good as expected. I have high expectations, is true. If you compare the Australia of today under Malcolm Turnbull with Australia of the 80's with Malcolm Frazer, Australia of the 80's win. There were classes of English beginners, advanced and intermediary, Hostels specialised in migrants, job programmes and extra money while you were searching for work and lived in a Hostel. In Australians hostels there were no fights. People were civilized. I remember having one the most fun time in my life while doing English classes, I became friend with the Dutch and teachers. We had a ball which lasted for 3 months. It was the Christmas time and to look for work was not appropriate I started dating something I did not do for a while. I was still depressed by my departure was a traumatic event and I needed catharsis. Remember crying for long time, two years. You can see my depression in the photos taken at the time. The first job I got, was with a German owner of a furniture company. It was not doing very well so he decided to retrench staff. The money was little. Next job was an assistant operator in a cable manufacturing plant. I did a lot of overtime and was paid a lot of money. The factory was taken to China, eventually. Today I do not expect anything in life like I did then when I was a refugee. A good capitalist system, was not to be. I am more developed today then yesterday. In my 20's I decided to work and enjoy life as much as possible. I could not get into courses I wanted. I started with mathematics and left it doing one subject at a time so that is why it took me so long to finish the course. No houses, no marriages and no commitments. I did my best with the knowledge of the time.

CHAPTER VIII

DISCOVERING PSYCHOLOGY

Discovering psychology to me means acquiring enough knowledge in order to apply it to your self. And I did that. All my life I believed I cannot change that I was born like that. It was fantastic to change even if it took 3-4 years for self esteem to be developed. My changes were partial, it takes 7 years to be changed, it was a mistake of mine. I had to go back to revise the stuff I knew and reimplemented. Too much fun not enough work. At the time I had a relationship which did not work so I thought the counsellor would turn it around for better. I asked a counsellor to help me but my partner did not want a relationship. Why spend so much time together if you do not want a relationship. She only wanted sex. In the same period I saw a psychologist for anxiety which has been with me for years. The psychologist was fighting with the counsellor so there was not so much progress and I was in the middle being referred by the social worker. I was not getting anywhere. I decided to take the side of the counsellor which in the end proved to be the wrong decision. The psychologist diary was full for 2 days seeing 16 people and she was a part time practitioner. I decided to change myself with no help form others. I had to read books and a lot of books in self-help areas.

In the same period, I had done a course in personal development for 3 weeks, run by Centrelink, it was good and proved to be helpful. With the help of Centrelink I started to turn my life around. At the back of a self-help book there were 100 books to read and decided to read them for the years to come. There was no other way. If you ask me if it was hard to read and do 100 books, I say yes. But also realise that I need to be a life time reader and learner in order to excel in life. So, reading 100 books will not do.

In 1995 after brief introduction into poker machines I had become a poker machines addict. Because I was addicted to gaming machines the transition to poker machines was easy. It provides the same set of grooves on the brain and that makes the transition fast. The addiction with poker machines proved to be a long battle. I used to spend 3 -4 hours in the venues. Next I went up to ten and the weekends. The luck was, that I never had too much money. So, they could not get so much from me. I was so excited about the machines liked the game features and figures and colours a lot. I was turned on when I went to the Venue, before doing anything I was going to jump over the machines, and then say Hello to stuff and ask for drinks

At the time I write this book, I have not touched the poker machines for 6 years. Not that it is bed, but is my goal never to play ongoing and replace the addiction with something which is more fulfilling. Write books, play guitar, painting or anything else which is constructed and away from poker machines. I have become an authority in addiction and self-publish my first book 'Addictions, the myth, how to conquer them' because it is a myth. Gambling Venues have done a lot of damage to the social strata, in particular the poor people. Some of them lost their houses, family, savings and even committed suicide. The Government cannot and will not get rid of poker machines. They are here to stay. So, the next best thing is to replace them with a healthy addiction and to realize that addictions are not bed. They are given to you by the mind and everybody is addicted unless he/she falls in love with another member of the human race.

I become good at meditation, 15 seconds. I become more and more loving. I used to help others as well. I worked on my energies and every month in every month I would have more and more energy. Being dependant like many of us, I went to see a psychologist even if the help was not there. These psychologists seem do not do much apart from bits here and there. They would not help, they would not run a course in dependencies. So much abuse of position. I could not believe that they would not run a course in dependencies with so many people thinking about suicide.

I let my family know about my discovery of self-esteem and psychology in general, but they did not appreciate that. My father, was not home very often. He was spending his time with the friends from work. My mother was at home and took care of us the best she could. My parents felt they were good parents. Despite the good parenting they have done, I was having difficulties in my life. I was withdrawn and antisocial.

In comparison my sister spent most of her time with the my parents. Even when she was married. I believe she did not have problems during this because she did not try to do anything. She was also sick a lot of the time.

As I previously mentioned I arrived in Australia in 1981, and rejected for studying full time in my Austudy application, I decided to take life easy and enjoy it in the 20's. Leave everything for the 30's. Also, I was never keen in pure mathematics subjects they would do in the first and second year of study. In 1989 I decided to take things seriously to do and finish my first degree. Looking for work is another desire of mine, but it was recession when I finished my first degree in 1990. It was difficult to find a job. I went and did the fourth year in statistics but still no luck in finding work. In psychology I was doing fine, but not in the job field. In 1996 the last year with a reasonable job, worked with BOC managers. A good job is a challenging job which pays well and you get the social skills required for life. Any way an employment is not about money only, you need to get something more from the job. Most of the jobs were temporary work and in the call center position, jobs for the egos.

Jobs have an effect on people, spending a lot of time at work is normal to affect you. Talking about jobs, I know a lot of people who have a very good knowledge of psychology but they do not practice what they preach. Some of them, having more knowledge then me. The more contribution we make as human beings the faster we change the monster world we live in. There are currently 15 million people who die every year, more than people die in wars.

CHAPTER IX

SAVING MY FATHER

Throughout my life I have seen a lot of lives lost, I can recall my first motorcycle. I had bought a Honda, very nice 125cc 4 speeds and 4 strokes. I have parked it outside and nothing could happen to my bike. When I woke up in the morning the bike was not there and the keys to the motorcycle, disappeared. In the morning I heard police at the door and the Police wanted to talk to me. Your friend had an accident on your motorbike in a collision with a car and he is dead. He lost his helmet and hit the car at 120 kmh speed. He was killed instantly You can say there is a bit of karma involved, but anyway. Anyway a loss of life is a loss of life, and it was the first one I encountered. His family came from Romania to see the funeral. I do not know who to blame, the car, or motorbike, but the car was at fault. Another, loss of life was the sister of my 'girlfriend' Annabel. At a high speed she was in a car which swerved and hit another car. She died instantly. This is my second accident involving someone close. For a couple of years I went out with an Italian/Australian. It was a relationship which it did not turn out very well. I did not want to get married. She had 2 brothers and 2 other sisters. One of them was quite beautiful, but died in a car accident. It seems like all the people close to me are going. Another guy I lived with myself, has a heart attack he was only 45 years old. He was actually very nice and helpful person. I recall another guy to died of heart attack. A guy who I met at the cable factory. We established connection again after few years. He was known to my parents because he spoke to them on my behalf when he went to Romania. He was very agitated when I met him. I knew he suffered from anxiety but did not expect him to die. He ended his life in heart failure under very a strong anxiety attack. I asked him to change because it was possible, but he refused. Through him I met his wife who by now was a widow. We started having coffee and from there a relationship was developed. She had 2 children and her parents were brought here by her husband.my friend. The relationship did not work, we were not compatible. This was something at the time I could not handle Also I do not like the fighting, I am a peaceful person, She wanted her parents to live with us, something which I did not agree with. So, in this case I accepted the Australian way of growing up where you are encouraged to build your own life. I had to assert myself. Something which I did not do at the time. Because of lack of assertion, I could not get what I wanted from the relationship. I had a good relationship with her son, something which I enjoyed a lot of time. I remember well there was an international diaspora taking place in Bucharest, year 2000.

As a representative of the current diaspora in Melbourne she was asked to leave the country and go to the meeting. At the same time my father had cancer of the prostate. He did not look that bad, but he had cancer. Me and my girlfriend had a meeting with him in Bucharest, because I could not stay longer. He had a psychological problem. He did not feel good enough because both of his kids were not married. I had no intention of getting married, maybe my sister had. I explained to him that marriages do not work these days. People need to be committed and that is not something they do. Marriage is not a measure of worth but who you are. He accepted my message in 2 weeks his bleeding was stopped. He was cured. He explained to his doctors that he had a radish which helped him to get rid of the cancer and of course they would not believe. Cancer is psychological. My sister got married after that. So, everything was better. I have to be very sure I can marry, buy anyway I am here for my mission, not marriage. I had to let go of the relationship. I manage to do it in the end. This family was Jewish with lots of desires. They emigrated from Ukraine and being Jewish they had a hard time. From Ukraine on one side and from Romanians on the other side. When the relationship finished I was very happy because I was out of a relationship where there were incompatibilities. I did not feel healthy at the time.

My father died at the age of 91. He was crying a lot and he did not face death with peace it was a tumultuous. He died of age, but he did not give up leaving.

CHAPTER X

GETTING ALONG

I know I could get along with people and believe in my life. I did not sleep in the right places. Every time there was recession, my life would become hard and money hard to get. the places to sleep was according to the current situation at the time. As soon as recession would come a bungalow would help me with accommodation. The one in Glen Waverley was a good example. The owner was a Shri Lankan and I did not get along well with him because I did not hold my own. I remember asking him for references and he would give me a hard time. I was looking for a rent reference not personal. Before him, I had a 2-bedroom apartment in Clayton. That was nice. Whenever I wanted somebody, and felt alone, I would rent a room. As soon as recession would come I moved to a bungalow in Glen Waverley, where the place was just bearable, and I could save money. Eventually I got an apartment in Armadale where the place was just bearable and big enough. I did not pay the rent on time and the owner wanted me out. It was hard for him to get me out because the Real Estate lady had a soft spot for me. I wanted to live in the inner suburb and Armadale, was one for me. As rent was not paid on time I moved out eventually.

This is the year of RMIT, where I did my fourth year. The subject marks should have been much higher, but because I did not get well with the lecturers were just passes. I managed to finish and started job hunting. I was not good at taking the opportunities and the good jobs were passing me. Even these days when something or someone is presented to me I do not take it. Eventually I end up in the back of the shops in a small place. The rent is cheap and also the privacy is good. You could sing and play guitar at any time without offending anybody. I repainted the place, polished the floor and fixed the shower. It ended up being OK. Getting along with the Real Estate was another story. They would not give me the credit for what I was. They wanted to be boss, but I did not agree. So, we ended up fighting for years. the owner of the shop was selfish and a bimbo. He did not give me any credit at all. I was OK with women who would take their place during the week. I guess this was something. I got a next door neighbour to the right of me, who was the same. He was the same, no credit. I believe in general people do not give. Because they are selfish. In 2003 I did a long contract, one year with immigration department, the language center in a position of call center operator. After an interview the manager felt sorry for me (he shouldn't have) and he gave me a job, I was happy with what I had and the call center positions is not something I fancy, Because they were all call center operation I decided to take them on. I was power struggling with every one of them 60 people. Eventually they hired permanent staff and got rid of the casual people. The money was good for unqualified people, just answer the call. I changed my self to an alternating shift 12 hours per day where the money was more and probably spent on gambling. In the first week the team leader said he was going to kick me out, it did not eventuate. I was warned again about being fired and it did not happened. That was a bad decision to do a 12 hours shift lost a lot of energy of which I only know now.

In 2004 they refurbished the shop as well as the back in Elsternwick. I Managed to sleep some extra nights because I could not find a place at that price. Eventually I moved to a rooming house in Caulfield, but it was not so bad. You were not sharing anything but you could not have a kitchen. The owner transformed the whole place into a place for students where he could charge more and make more money. He also had a factory of air conditioners. Again, I did not get on well with the owner and the new administrator. My memory is not that good but eventually I got a room in a pub on Chapel street. It was cheap, and everything was close by. Most of the noise was from the bands which would play on the weekend. You had to get out on Chapel street, everything was shaky. I tried to assert myself with the manager but that did not work. His son did not like people over 40 he was just 21. Eventually I left the room and got a place in a community housing, a bedsitting room with everything supplied in terms of furniture, Before this, I worked with Vodafone as a call center Operator, a job from hell. I started with 25 hours per week and it was good because you would not lose energy and at that time Vodafone was a "New Age" company. The company was not interested in money that much but in making the customers happy. And I enjoy that it was in my alley. But at once the mother company in England decides to replace the CEO with a main stream CEO and the company became no different from any other mobile companies. They were interested in money only. My stupid decision was to ask for 50 hours per week not 20. At 50 hours per week my energy went from 10 hours per day to 3 hours per day. Again, I fought with the majority because I was in a velvet Suit. I was not the only one who had power struggling there, were another two women. The boss was gay and he was a she. He did not enjoy anybody better then him, The team leader. was actually speaking a lot about me believing that I am a mature person. One day two team leaders were hired, and I got one of them. He started asserting over me and also, he was picking on me. Finally, after picking on me they found mistakes in my job and they fired me.

I had low energy in myself because I did not know that I lose energy in call centersI got the housing community apartment and moved in with virtually nothing. There were 3 people working in the office, the manager was one of them. I could not get along with her for some reasons, just I need to reiterate here I am self-esteem not a man I call myself loverman. I do not like to dominate. With the other 2 women I was OK. Which is an achievement. I started to get along with people. At the community housings everybody was sick and kept to themselves. The manager wanted to lock me up, this is not the first person to do that. She talked to the GP and the GP (general practitioner) said no. He knew she did not like me because I was a man. Also, I gave her the process of death which is a growing process. She went further to the management of community centers. The answer was no again, Eventually she went to Kevin Rudd, and guess what, he knew about me because I made contact with him regarding the economy. And he said, man with such a passion cannot be locked up. I do not know at this hour, what happened to her. I know she left the job and it was for the rough people, as I said to her. She tried to become friends with some of my friends from the hospital, but I said no. First time I got her back. She was screaming like a tiger and she gave me hard time every time she met me. I have made a pass at her, but she said no, and then I moved on. Next, I will be moving in to a Bungalow at the back of the rooming house. The community house was noisy and full of trades people. Once a week. The alarm was going all the time while cooking. You could not have a proper sleep.

Chapter XI

GAINING 85% OF ENERGY IN THE BATTERY AND THEN LOSE IT ALL IN 2 YEARS

T he critical and vital message I would like to convey is to manage your energies. Managing your energies is the most important factor in your life. A lot of people would say you need time to do a lot of things. There is time to do the most important things but never enough to do all the tasks. You need to know where you gain energy and where you lose energy. You need to make the boring 'sleep' in your life important. The sleep is very important. I spent years in cheap places where I had a lot of noise while sleeping. I could not get the proper sleep. The people you hang around with will give energy or take your energy. The job you perform will give you energy or lose energy. The rental market in Melbourne is high for the moment, and is hard to obtain a private place at a reasonable price. Despite all this you need to sleep. Low level of energy will make you unhealthy and you need to see doctors to get well. To be happy you need energy, to go to work you will need energy. Even when you sleep you need a bit of energy for the organs. In general, the level of energy in society is low at about 50-60%, not enough to be happy. One more reason to change the world is to receive a better level of energy from the superconscious. Maybe we will receive food through energies, who knows?!! Using affirmations, catharsis, meditations, cognitive thinking for anxiety, dealing with depression, dealing with worries, helped me acquired a good level of energy, energy which never had. This was still not enough, I fell in love with the psychologist, this pushed my energies right up. So much that I could not see ageing. My eyes were healthy like they should be and their movement was fast. There was no eye problem.

The energies discovered from psychology were good, but the energy from falling in love with a flower, they were equally good. The problem with the psychologist was that it was a one sided relationship. To fall in love at the age of forty was something, but the love was not reciprocated. I did not understand what equally means. If I look back, I was a fool because the person was not a flower, and that changed the relationship. In terms of energies my battery was good, at 85% which is high but there was no relationship. The relationship ended because we were not equal. By that she meant equal on the dominant pole. I thought she meant I am a refugee, did not have a good job, have an accent. At the time I could not see the psychologist for what she was. Today I do not value those types of relationships. I would have put it on hold, no close relationship. I have no close relationship with people into power. The book which I copied and sent to her was returned and marked the end of the relationship. I was depressed for a while but in a way realized it was a one-way relationship.

In the call center position if not ½ of my energy was wasted at least 1/3 lost. Despite all these loses my energy was good. I started getting panic attacks while by myself, scared that I will lose my dole, it was a time when the government was attacking a lot of people on welfare. Between 10 pm and 11 pm I was receiving numerous panic attacks, I lost 20 kg in 3 weeks. It was hard to control the panic attacks. I went to the local counselling service and they told me if I genuinely look for work they will not put me on the street. That fixed the panic attacks. 60% of energy was gone, the only thing left was 25%. I was still not getting it, I was losing energy in call centers. I was hired with Vodafone.as I mentioned. I had to do it they would have cut me off the dole. After 50 hours per week my energies went down to 12.5 %.From 25% battery it goes down to 12%. Which is low, and you can hardly get out of bed, and fulfils Centre Link activities as I was back on the dole.

While on zero energy, when I could not get out of bed, I decided to see the health professionals because I cannot heal myself. After one and a half years of seeing the doctors it was decided that I have chronic fatigue. A condition where you have low level of energy and not known by all doctors. Mine did not know the condition so I needed to convince him that is so. After six months he gave up. Today chronic fatigue is still not recognised specifically by small practises. Not having contacted specialist clinicians my idea was that the muscle loss from panic attacks needed to be fixed in order to have the chronic fatigue dealt with.

While in community housing I had an anxiety attack which was very hard to stop and I lost 20 kilograms in 3 days. I went to Alfred Hospital to ask for help. I wanted to monitor my system while in anxiety attacks. They helped me for a night and the anxiety attacks stopped. This time I decided to stop rebuilding my body, it was like a fat person losing weight and then putting it back on, only it was the other direction around.

What I had was not depending on the body but on the battery of the subconscious mind which needed replenishing. In less than 2 years, 2003-2004 the battery was brought from 85% to 12%.

CHAPTER XII

LIFE IN ROOMING HOUSES
AND THE BUNGALOW

As I said I decided to leave the community house, because of the noise for a bungalow. It was not enough money to move out to a more appropriate place.

I thought I would have privacy. I was wrong. Because the place was made of wood, people would talk to you via the wall. I do not know how this is exactly because I do not talk through the walls or door even if they are made of wood. So, I had to gain my privacy, meaning people would not talk to me around my place of existence. There were 10 rooming houses and I had to convince the whole lot that I had to get the required privacy. At one time I thought I would get it. Even if they said I was going to get the privacy they did not mean it. They did not mean to give me privacy, it was all a hoax. They never had any intentions and I realize that I had to leave. So, for nearly 10 months I had to fight and did not get the privacy. I had to leave the place, a very hard task because of lack of energy and money. This period of time was very hard because of chronic fatigue, every day I had anxiety. My life was under threat and I did not believe the police would take my side because I was very sick. I was afraid I would be lynched by the people at the house. In this period of time, I was also monitored. Every move, any decision I would make would be monitored to see if I was as good as I thought I was. Every situation handled I used to get a pass or not a pass. I was not proud of the monitoring system, especially when they knew my life was in danger. They did not intervene and also took the side of the rooming house.

The place was expensive at the time, I was a smoker and picked up cigarettes butts at the Pub at 3 o'clock in the morning. The electricity was high from week to week and I had to save and plan. The energy bills at the time were high because, I was sleeping during the day and I was awake during the night.

I went to see my GP for a place to sleep and a bottle of Temaze. The doctor denied my housing request but gave me a bottle of sleeping pills. I met the doctor in 1995 and was with him for nearly 20 years. The guy was pretty good at holding his own.

I decided to go and see how many friends I had left in my life. Not many. I took most of the essential items in a bag and left the place for the Alfred Hospital. The idea was to stay 2 or 3 days in the Alfred to regain energy and move on to another place of residence. After spending a night at emergency the doctor decided not to take me in, because I was supposed to take not to be given. After being through so much I had to take, surely something is wrong with the health system. People need another system.

I was on the street with no energy no money and no place to sleep. I thought it was unavoidable to think about ending my life. But all of the sudden the Alfred Hospital CAT team picks me up and they put me in to the psychiatric ward and my life keeps going. I still hid my bottled for later use, in case I needed a number of pills.

CHAPTER XIII

HOSPITAL, SRS, COMMUNITY CARE UNIT

This is the first contact with the psychiatric unit at the Alfred, not taking into account my previous encounter with the CAT team when I was depressed or when I had an anxiety attack. We are going to have some time together. Because of them I am still alive today. Trialling medication is a painful process and sometimes very hurtful. Until now I only used Paroxetine for anxiety attacks and depression and iron for anaemia, which took 8 months to heal. When I was with the rooming house bungalow I had anaemia. It was hard to deal with anaemia. I got it while I carried my belongings from community housing to the bungalow. It was very cold during the night and as I used all my energies. I did not have any left for the warming of my body. Because I had a flu they would not analyse my blood. A GP I know would not do it, and the Alfred Hospital after 4 hours of waiting, would not do it either. They even picked on me and ask how can a guy with extreme chronic fatigue can wait for so long. I did a trial and error in the supermarket and find out the Iron level was low. Took 2 tablets a day but I was slow in recovering so I took them before food when the stomach was empty and it worked even if it caused constipation

It took 8 months to heal anaemia. I did not know at the time, would have probably taken my life. Any way I felt the building of the channels and layers in my body. The emotions in the mind were out somewhere that I do not recall. The channels and layers were for energy carrying, I remember the life line coming back home. In this period, I was looking for a sleeping pill. And tried melatonin 5 milligrams. I could not move for 2 hours the only thing going were my eye movements and I thought I was going to die. Now at the Alfred was the time to trial numerous medications. It Took 6 weeks of trial to come up with my medication. I got Seroquel which is a good medication for sleep. I also tried respiradon, as antipsychotic medication, in Tablets and Injections. I could not walk properly so, it was dropped after a few trials. I try different antidepressant medication and anti-anxiety. like Effexor (headaches), escitalopram (blockage of energy), clozapine (antipsychotic) and others including injections. The main side effects were blocking and hard to walk. At the time I was followed by the media and the money had to be kept by someone you can trust from the Alfred Hospital; my friends. It is believed that the superconscious solution was stuffed up. I do not believe, persuading the government is a hard task which lasts a while and you need patience and perseverance until they will say yes, It was believed that I could not take care of myself in the sense of medication, so I was put on the "community treatment order". It meant that the doctors will take care of my medicine. Currently the number of people in Victoria on "community treatment orders" are doubled of any other states. It should not be like that. If I believe that a medication is not good and do not like it should not be taken. I get put on injections where people will force to inject. Currently my medication is fine and does not need to be changed. As soon as you are hospitalized at the psychiatric intake, they will change the medication because you are on a "community treatment order". Even if you are not on community treatment order they will put you back at the slightest mistake. It is also something of control. You control the medication, you control the individual. They brought internet to look at the medication you take. As I said the system is for psychiatrist it should be for the patient like the private system.

I was also monitored by people at high level, similar to the bungalow in Saint Kilda only a different team. Again, how I handle the situation, how I go in various scenarios and how I handle the pressure. My level of energy was low and I did not have the right medication., I found the monitoring hard. At one time, I did not have any energy at all. It was hard to get up from the bed. I decided to take my own life with an overdose of sleeping pills which I hid outside the hospital. I took them and fell asleep. I could not take my life. I slept for 6 hours which gave me energy for 2-3 hours a day. That was my first time I tried to take my life out of three.

At The Alfred, I was supposed to be given an isolated one bedroom flat. It did not eventuate because of my failure to get up, I should had used my spare energy in the battery, energy of which I had some. Always keep some in reserve. Some people suggested that I should go back to the bungalow and fight. How can I fight with ten people. It was a suicide. I decided to keep going with the mission and the things I was supposed to do, the things I was sent here in this world to do. The sleeping pills gave me a new life. There was light at the end of the tunnel.

At the time I was not able to cook, not able to clean and I was full of anxiety. The food in hospital is not that good it needs a revision. It made me feel sick. The stool was hard and became full of haemorrhoids. People were screaming during the night, making the sleep harder. Anyway, it took a while to accommodate with the situation, to see how the psychiatric hospital is working. It is not like the general hospital where everybody is there to help you. As I said it is about the psychiatrists. Unlike a private hospital where you are the patient .and attention is around you. Something needs to be done so the patient is the centre. Also, there are people who have been sick for 10,15 and even 20 years. Something needs to be done about this as well, too much pain and suffering. The new system should take care of the very sick people, people who have been sick 10 to 20 years and put them in special divisions run by the best doctors.

The places in hospital are scarce, talking about the public hospital, so there was arrangement for me to go. Destination houses where people clean and feed meals to you. At the time when I was referred to houses SRS (special recreative services) following rental payment and medicines paid there was still some money left for you to feel good. This time however the rents are so high that is nothing left in your pocket, and what is the use of living?!!! Something needs to be done for these people like subsidized rent or some money of some kind.

The SRS houses were a horror, people used to fight all day. There was no quiet place to sleep. Also, the place was expensive for what it provided. The food was worse than the hospital, so bad that I was forced to do the haemorrhoid operation at the Alfred Hospital. I had to wait 6 weeks. It got so bad that I decided to take my life again, this time there was no light at the end of tunnel and the only thing I was thinking about was the operation. I took the scissors and umbrella and in the back of houses I tried to cut my wrist. It did not work. I had to use something sharper, like blades. This was the second try at taking my life. The next one would be more in the future. The Manager of the SRS did a good job she bandaged me and called for the ambulance. At the Hospital they did another bandage and put glue on the wound, It took 2 months for the scar to disappear. They send me back during the night with a cab voucher.

All the above bought me some time to have the operation performed. Once the operation was done the mind was back to normal not obsessed with the haemorrhoid. Because I had the flu just before the operation, I got the 'munchies', lucky I had some money in the superannuation account and for 2 months I eat and eat. Exactly when I finished my little money I had it was decided I had to move. I was glad I would be send to CCU (community care unit) which will be my home for nearly a year and where I could clean and cook. It was to be the best place for a while. And as usual I expected more then I got and become disappointed.

The place was run by Doctors and nurses 24 hours a day it was meant to be like a rehabilitation centre where people learn again to cook and clean. The step up before being released by yourself. I was very close from being cured of my chronic fatigue. The mind was broken in to pieces and to bring it back I needed an intense feeling. I did not have any anxiety at the time, as I currently have. Because

I am by myself it is hard for me to cure. It was decided that I should go because I could not do my activities, 3 a week. I was only doing 2.

At CCU I had problems in the sense that I was suicidal most of the time. The Alfred Hospital did a good job for me every time I was suicidal they would push me up Also the CCU did the same thing. I think in 9 months they pushed me up 20 times and I think it was getting too much for the Alfred Hospital. I borrowed a rope and found my trees in the closed park. Never got close to use it.

It was luck for me. A 'transitional one bedroom flat' became available, otherwise I would not have a place to sleep. Going back to SRS was not a solution and I am glad the case manager understood that. After a few interviews I was given the flat with the condition that see the nurses every week. Transitional flat means you stay there until an offer of housing comes up, usually high-rise apartment. My body skeleton was not good following basketball in my high school years. I needed a one bedroom flat to be at a ground level. I could not get that.

CHAPTER XIV

ONE BEDROOM FLAT AND BOARDING HOUSE

M oving in the one bedroom flat has its own rewards. It was made by bricks, for the first time meant nobody could talk to me via the wall. For the first time I had only 7 neighbours. The rent was cheap and affordable. It was at the ground floor which helped with the other conditions as well. It was luck to find a place made of brick in South Yarra, also hard work from CCU, even if they did not give me the support and privacy I required. I was given a flat with privacy. I also had my name down for a place with Housing Commission. They can take anywhere between 2 years to 10 years in the inner suburbs as I wanted.

The noise from the street took its toll on me, I had to see a psychologist to sooth the body hurt by the noise. It helped to know that noise does not kill and is harmless. It helped with further living under noise. In the beginning, it did not affect me After a while it got in to me. In 2 years of living I had the following: water pipe renewal, another water pipe faulty, use bitumen on the surface, house construction, another house construction, apartment redone, apartment refurbished, windows replacing, bitumen replacing twice, big water pipes done this was in 2 years.

I used to go to the Alfred Hospital and to short term accommodation Park. The team assigned to me was not that good. At one time they stopped me going to the hospital believing that I have the edge over hospital being suicidal. In, other words they have to take me to the hospital. They have no choice in that. I wish they were in my shoes. For the third time in 5 years I tried to take my life again. It was too much, there was no help and no light at the end of the tunnel. The caring team was cold that did not help. The chronic fatigue can be cured, I know how to get rid of it, but I feel like giving up. Not worth going through a hard time, to get a cold response from people. Again, an overdose of sleeping pills. This time I took more than the last time. Still no luck. I get up like nothing happened. It was suggested that taking your life is not an easy thing, especially when you do not want to feel pain. I believe that in all these years the chronic fatigue was not cured because of the accommodation problems faced by Australia, particular in Sydney and Melbourne, due to a high demand of cheap places to live.

Because of my age or because I had support form MST (mobile support team of Alfred Hospital) I was offered a place to sleep by The Housing Commission (old name) who was at High Rise where people leave close to each other and scream at each other. I was not actually on immediate list and I had to prove that by asking for a ground floor flat with medium rise building not high rise. An approval for the medium rise was given. So, the refusal of the property given was not recorded,

With the tricks acquired from a friend who knows how to look for a place to live, I start chasing accommodation. First on application and be sure that the place you would like to live in is the place you apply for. Done that and after 3 serious applications a place in South Yarra was offered. A rooming house, even better you have your own kitchen and living room, you live in South Yarra with just 4 friends. I gave up smoking which is probably the most expensive thing in the world. After 39 years I gave up smoking. Save money for the bond, save money for the furniture, I had not had my furniture for long time. I do not know how many years. The place found is as good as any housing commissions. It is not as bad as it sounds. You have your own privacy, and the noise does not bother me. I found the flat in the rooming houses just before I was given another flat from Housing Commission and I was going to say no so I would have been evicted and left on the street from the current brick flat.

CHAPTER XV

FIGHTS AND SOME SITUATIONS

U sually I live in the moment I have my day set up, so I only need to worry about the day. In today's world I believe you only get moments and relationships, but relationships are something you need to work hard into maintain. So, living in the moment is paramount to me. Because of this it is harder to remember things in the past, and requires some phenomenal help. There are certain important parts of myself which I do not remember very well so I build a chapter called Fights and Situations which describes me on certain part of the journey. Do not take it wrongly, it is still part of myself but they are fragments of my remembering.

While in secondary school in the late years of studies with a bad kidney I was dismissed from the lessons in sport because I was incapacitated. The teacher was new, and I did not turn up, he bashed me and broke my year for not turning up to be there. I told my parents, and they complained to the director.

I had some connections through my mathematics teachers and landed up in a hospital run by the brother of Nicolae Ceausescu. This is when I had my kidney problems. Because they knew I was referred by him the staff gave me a hard time. They used to wake me up in the morning to help the nurses distribute medication. The food was a disaster, all sugar and gem for 2 weeks. I could not get in touch with my parents, because they would say to them everything is fine, we take care of him. Even my x-ray results were no good for any conclusion.

While with kidney problems I used to see various specialists and most of them would say that my life will be ended soon I did no buy that and on the happiness scale I was good. Only one doctor said he looks happy, so I believe he will recover. I recovered in 2 years with vitamins and antibiotic for the infection. I finally got the attention I needed,

Because the high school was part of the system of Education and also the other half was from the Transport system we were getting paid for the high marks. In other words if you have marks over a certain trash hold you will get money. And they were very good I could go out I could buy the clothes I wanted and also an electric guitar. Money at the age of 14 th year.

In elementary school but more in High School I used to study mathematics. Whatever the teachers would teach in class it was not good enough to do much. I had to do other things. I used put thought into private mathematic at a higher level and also do a lot of exercises from various books. There was competition for mathematics in high school where I used to prepare myself. In Australia I did not take it too seriously that is why it took me a while to finish.

I was in last year of high school and what was going to unfold was something of that would affect me all my life. I fall on the cement with my left hip and all of sudden my hip was in pain. It was not until I was applying for a USA immigration visa that I found out that there was a mark on my hip. Any way mark or no mark, I could go and live my life normally without being too affected. But this was not to be. While at CCU (community care unit) they put me at the first level and I explained to them that I needed to be at ground floor because of my hip. They would not do anything about it, they would tell me to ignore it. Well soon after that my hip felt like it came out of the socket and I mean the right hip, not the affected left hip. As soon as I sat up I had problems with ankles, So, one little bump will do tremendous damage in my life. I am currently waiting for a knee operation, another part in my life where the skeleton is not working properly.

I know that teachers have brought life in our little souls while young. We used to like some of them we used to dislike some of them and others we did not care. Some of them from a sexual point of view we use to like. I remember my mathematics teacher from primary school and my Romanian language teacher in high school. I had a crush on them. There were also the sports teacher and the German Language teacher who was unusual blonde. We even used mirrors to look under teachers' skirt. Looking back in time I could not help myself in seeing the fun we had while growing up.

www.ingramcontent.com/pod-product-compliance
Lightning Source LLC
Chambersburg PA
CBHW031235120626
46545CB00003B/1135